The Wedding of

Bride

Groom

Wedding Date:

This Wedding Planner
Belongs To:

_____

Wedding Plans

Grooms Parents

Mother of the Groom

Father of the Groom

Brides Parents

Mother of the Bride

Father of the Bride

Plans & Ideas
Thoughts

Plans & Ideas

Must Haves

Important Dates

DATE:	DATE:	DATE:	REMINDERS
DATE:	DATE:	DATE:	
DATE:	DATE:	DATE:	NOTES
DATE:	DATE:	DATE:	
DATE:	DATE:	DATE:	

Important Dates

DATE:	DATE:	DATE:	REMINDERS
DATE:	DATE:	DATE:	
DATE:	DATE:	DATE:	NOTES
DATE:	DATE:	DATE:	
DATE:	DATE:	DATE:	

Wedding Budget *Expense* MANAGER

CATEGORY/ITEMS	BUDGET	ACTUAL COST	BALANCE

Wedding Budget Checklist

CATEGORY	BUDGET	ACTUAL COST	DEPOSIT	BALANCE

Notes

Planning Snapshot

CEREMONY EXPENSE TRACKER

	BUDGET	COST	DEPOSIT	BALANCE	DUE DATE
OFFICIANT GRATUITY					
MARRIAGE LICENSE					
VENUE COST					
FLOWERS					
DECORATIONS					
RINGS					

NOTES & Reminders

NOTES & REMINDERS

RECEPTION EXPENSE TRACKER

	BUDGET	COST	DEPOSIT	BALANCE	DUE DATE
VENUE FEE					
CATERING/FOOD					
BAR/BEVERAGES					
CAKE/CUTTING FEE					
DECORATIONS					
RENTALS/EXTRAS					
BARTENDER/STAFF					

NOTES & More

SPECIAL REMINDERS

Travel Plans

PARENTS TRAVEL EXPENSE TRACKER					
	BUDGET	COST	DEPOSIT	BALANCE	DUE DATE
TRAVEL PLANS					
AIRLINE					
HOTEL					
CAR RENTAL					

NOTES & Reminders

SPECIAL REMINDERS

Notes:

Travel Plans

TRAVEL EXPENSE TRACKER

	BUDGET	COST	DEPOSIT	BALANCE	DUE DATE
TRAVEL PLANS					
AIRLINE					
HOTEL					
CAR RENTAL					

NOTES & Reminders

SPECIAL REMINDERS

Notes:

Rehearsal Dinner Plans

Rehearsal Dinner Budget

CATEGORY	BUDGET	ACTUAL COST	DEPOSIT	BALANCE

Rehearsal Venue Planner

Venue Planning Details

Rehearsal Meal Planner

REHEARSAL EXPENSE TRACKER

ITEM/PURCHASE	STATUS ✓	DATE PAID	TOTAL COST
☐			
☐			
☐			
☐			
☐			

NOTES & REMINDERS

TOTAL COST:

Planning Details

Rehearsal Dinner Guests

NAME	ADDRESS	PHONE#	# IN PARTY	RSVP ✔

Rehearsal Dinner Guests

NAME	ADDRESS	PHONE#	# IN PARTY	RSVP ✔

Rehearsal Dinner Guests

NAME	ADDRESS	PHONE#	# IN PARTY	RSVP ✔

Contact List

NAME	PHONE #	EMAIL	ADDRESS

Notes

SPECIAL REMINDERS

Planning Snapshot

WEDDING ATTIRE EXPENSE TRACKER

	BUDGET	COST	DEPOSIT	BALANCE	DUE DATE
WEDDING ATTIRE					
SHOES/HEELS					
TUX RENTAL					
SUIT					
SHOES					
ALTERATION COSTS					

NOTES & Reminders

NOTES & REMINDERS

TRANSPORTATION EXPENSE TRACKER

	BUDGET	COST	DEPOSIT	BALANCE	DUE DATE
LIMO RENTAL					
VALET PARKING					
VENUE TRANSPORTATION					
AIRPORT TRANSPORTATION					
OTHER:					
OTHER:					
OTHER:					

NOTES & More

SPECIAL REMINDERS

Wedding Attire Planner

WEDDING ATTIRE EXPENSE TRACKER

ITEM/PURCHASE	STATUS ✓	DATE PAID	TOTAL COST
☐			
☐			
☐			
☐			
☐			

NOTES & REMINDERS

TOTAL COST:

Notes:

Wedding Attire Details

Planning Snapshot

EXPENSE TRACKER			
	APPOINTMENT DATE	SALON	COST
HAIR			
MAKEUP			
MANI/PEDI			

NOTES & *Reminders*

SPECIAL REMINDERS

Notes:

....

....

....

....

....

Details

Catering Planner

CATERING EXPENSE TRACKER

ITEM/PURCHASE	STATUS ✓	DATE PAID	TOTAL COST
☐			
☐			
☐			
☐			
☐			

NOTES & REMINDERS	
	TOTAL COST:

Notes:

....

....

....

....

....

....

....

Caterer Planner Details

Entertainment Planner

ENTERTAINMENT EXPENSE TRACKER

ITEM/PURCHASE	STATUS ✓	DATE PAID	TOTAL COST
☐			
☐			
☐			
☐			
☐			

NOTES & REMINDERS

TOTAL COST:

Notes:

Love

Entertainment Details

Videographer Planner

VIDEOGRAPHER EXPENSE TRACKER

ITEM/PURCHASE	STATUS ✓	DATE PAID	TOTAL COST
☐			
☐			
☐			
☐			
☐			

NOTES & REMINDERS

TOTAL COST:

Notes:

....
....
....
....
....
....
....

Videographer Details

Photographer Planner

PHOTOGRAPHER EXPENSE TRACKER			
ITEM/PURCHASE	STATUS ✓	DATE PAID	TOTAL COST
☐			
☐			
☐			
☐			
☐			

NOTES & REMINDERS

TOTAL COST:

Notes:

Photographer Details

Florist Planner

FLORIST EXPENSE TRACKER

ITEM/PURCHASE	STATUS ✓	DATE PAID	TOTAL COST
☐			
☐			
☐			
☐			
☐			

NOTES & REMINDERS	
	TOTAL COST:

Notes:

Florist Planning Details

Extra Wedding Costs

MISC WEDDING EXPENSE TRACKER

ITEM/PURCHASE	STATUS ✓	DATE PAID	TOTAL COST
☐			
☐			
☐			
☐			
☐			

NOTES & REMINDERS

TOTAL COST:

Notes:

Misc Wedding Details

Bachelor Party Planner

EVENT DETAILS

DATE

TIME

VENUE

THEME

HOST

OTHER

SCHEDULE OF EVENTS

TIME	

GUEST LIST

FIRST NAME	LAST NAME	✔

SUPPLIES & SHOPPING LIST

- ☐
- ☐
- ☐
- ☐
- ☐
- ☐
- ☐
- ☐
- ☐
- ☐
- ☐
- ☐
- ☐
- ☐
- ☐
- ☐
- ☐

NOTES & REMINDERS

love

Honeymoon Plans & Ideas

Dreams

Honeymoon Plans Snapshot

HONEYMOON EXPENSE TRACKER					
	BUDGET	COST	DEPOSIT	BALANCE	DUE DATE
TRAVEL PLANS					
AIRLINE					
HOTEL					
CAR RENTAL					

NOTES & Reminders

SPECIAL REMINDERS

Notes:

Reception Planner

MEAL PLANNER IDEAS

HORS D'OEUVRES

1st COURSE:

3rd COURSE:

2nd COURSE:

4th COURSE:

Meal Planning Notes

Reception Planning Notes

Notes

Wedding Planning Notes

Notes

Groom's Planner

HAIR APPOINTMENT

SALON NAME	DATE	TIME	BOOKED FOR:	ADDRESS:
			☐	
			☐	
			☐	

	NOTES

TUX FITTING APPOINTMENT

BUSINESS NAME	DATE	TIME	BOOKED FOR:	ADDRESS:
			☐	
			☐	
			☐	

	NOTES

OTHER

BUSINESS NAME	DATE	TIME	BOOKED FOR:	ADDRESS:
			☐	
			☐	
			☐	

	NOTES

Weekly Wedding Planning

WEEK OF: _____

MONDAY

TUESDAY

WEDNESDAY

THURSDAY

FRIDAY

SATURDAY

WEDDING TO DO LIST

- ☐ _____
- ☐ _____
- ☐ _____
- ☐ _____
- ☐ _____
- ☐ _____
- ☐ _____
- ☐ _____
- ☐ _____
- ☐ _____
- ☐ _____
- ☐ _____
- ☐ _____
- ☐ _____
- ☐ _____
- ☐ _____
- ☐ _____
- ☐ _____

APPOINTMENTS & MEETINGS

DATE	TIME	VENDOR	PURPOSE

Weekly Wedding Planning

WEEK OF: _____

MONDAY

TUESDAY

WEDNESDAY

THURSDAY

FRIDAY

SATURDAY

WEDDING TO DO LIST

- [ ] _____
- [ ] _____
- [ ] _____
- [ ] _____
- [ ] _____
- [ ] _____
- [ ] _____
- [ ] _____
- [ ] _____
- [ ] _____
- [ ] _____
- [ ] _____
- [ ] _____
- [ ] _____
- [ ] _____
- [ ] _____
- [ ] _____
- [ ] _____

APPOINTMENTS & MEETINGS

DATE	TIME	VENDOR	PURPOSE

Weekly Wedding Planning

WEEK OF: _____

MONDAY

TUESDAY

WEDNESDAY

THURSDAY

FRIDAY

SATURDAY

WEDDING TO DO LIST

- [ ] _____
- [ ] _____
- [ ] _____
- [ ] _____
- [ ] _____
- [ ] _____
- [ ] _____
- [ ] _____
- [ ] _____
- [ ] _____
- [ ] _____
- [ ] _____
- [ ] _____
- [ ] _____
- [ ] _____
- [ ] _____
- [ ] _____
- [ ] _____

APPOINTMENTS & MEETINGS

DATE	TIME	VENDOR	PURPOSE

Weekly Wedding Planning

WEEK OF: _____

MONDAY

TUESDAY

WEDNESDAY

THURSDAY

FRIDAY

SATURDAY

WEDDING TO DO LIST

- ☐ _____
- ☐ _____
- ☐ _____
- ☐ _____
- ☐ _____
- ☐ _____
- ☐ _____
- ☐ _____
- ☐ _____
- ☐ _____
- ☐ _____
- ☐ _____
- ☐ _____
- ☐ _____
- ☐ _____
- ☐ _____
- ☐ _____

APPOINTMENTS & MEETINGS

DATE	TIME	VENDOR	PURPOSE

Weekly Wedding Planning

WEEK OF: _____

WEDDING TO DO LIST

- ☐ _____
- ☐ _____
- ☐ _____
- ☐ _____
- ☐ _____
- ☐ _____
- ☐ _____
- ☐ _____
- ☐ _____
- ☐ _____
- ☐ _____
- ☐ _____
- ☐ _____
- ☐ _____
- ☐ _____
- ☐ _____
- ☐ _____

MONDAY

TUESDAY

WEDNESDAY

THURSDAY

FRIDAY

SATURDAY

APPOINTMENTS & MEETINGS

DATE	TIME	VENDOR	PURPOSE

Weekly Wedding Planning

WEEK OF: _____

MONDAY

TUESDAY

WEDNESDAY

THURSDAY

FRIDAY

SATURDAY

WEDDING TO DO LIST

- [ ] _____
- [ ] _____
- [ ] _____
- [ ] _____
- [ ] _____
- [ ] _____
- [ ] _____
- [ ] _____
- [ ] _____
- [ ] _____
- [ ] _____
- [ ] _____
- [ ] _____
- [ ] _____
- [ ] _____
- [ ] _____

APPOINTMENTS & MEETINGS

DATE	TIME	VENDOR	PURPOSE

Weekly Wedding Planning

WEEK OF: _____

MONDAY

TUESDAY

WEDNESDAY

THURSDAY

FRIDAY

SATURDAY

WEDDING TO DO LIST

- [ ] _____
- [ ] _____
- [ ] _____
- [ ] _____
- [ ] _____
- [ ] _____
- [ ] _____
- [ ] _____
- [ ] _____
- [ ] _____
- [ ] _____
- [ ] _____
- [ ] _____
- [ ] _____
- [ ] _____
- [ ] _____
- [ ] _____
- [ ] _____

APPOINTMENTS & MEETINGS

DATE	TIME	VENDOR	PURPOSE

Weekly Wedding Planning

WEEK OF: _____

WEDDING TO DO LIST

- ☐ _____
- ☐ _____
- ☐ _____
- ☐ _____
- ☐ _____
- ☐ _____
- ☐ _____
- ☐ _____
- ☐ _____
- ☐ _____
- ☐ _____
- ☐ _____
- ☐ _____
- ☐ _____
- ☐ _____
- ☐ _____
- ☐ _____

MONDAY

TUESDAY

WEDNESDAY

THURSDAY

FRIDAY

SATURDAY

APPOINTMENTS & MEETINGS

DATE	TIME	VENDOR	PURPOSE

Weekly Wedding Planning

WEEK OF: _____

MONDAY

TUESDAY

WEDNESDAY

THURSDAY

FRIDAY

SATURDAY

WEDDING TO DO LIST

- [ ] _____
- [ ] _____
- [ ] _____
- [ ] _____
- [ ] _____
- [ ] _____
- [ ] _____
- [ ] _____
- [ ] _____
- [ ] _____
- [ ] _____
- [ ] _____
- [ ] _____
- [ ] _____
- [ ] _____
- [ ] _____

APPOINTMENTS & MEETINGS

DATE	TIME	VENDOR	PURPOSE

Weekly Wedding Planning

WEEK OF: _____

WEDDING TO DO LIST

- [ ] _____
- [ ] _____
- [ ] _____
- [ ] _____
- [ ] _____
- [ ] _____
- [ ] _____
- [ ] _____
- [ ] _____
- [ ] _____
- [ ] _____
- [ ] _____
- [ ] _____
- [ ] _____
- [ ] _____
- [ ] _____

MONDAY

TUESDAY

WEDNESDAY

THURSDAY

FRIDAY

SATURDAY

APPOINTMENTS & MEETINGS

DATE	TIME	VENDOR	PURPOSE

Weekly Wedding Planning

WEEK OF: _____

MONDAY

TUESDAY

WEDNESDAY

THURSDAY

FRIDAY

SATURDAY

WEDDING TO DO LIST

- ☐ _____
- ☐ _____
- ☐ _____
- ☐ _____
- ☐ _____
- ☐ _____
- ☐ _____
- ☐ _____
- ☐ _____
- ☐ _____
- ☐ _____
- ☐ _____
- ☐ _____
- ☐ _____
- ☐ _____
- ☐ _____
- ☐ _____

APPOINTMENTS & MEETINGS

DATE	TIME	VENDOR	PURPOSE

Weekly Wedding Planning

WEEK OF: _____

MONDAY

TUESDAY

WEDNESDAY

THURSDAY

FRIDAY

SATURDAY

WEDDING TO DO LIST

- ☐ _____
- ☐ _____
- ☐ _____
- ☐ _____
- ☐ _____
- ☐ _____
- ☐ _____
- ☐ _____
- ☐ _____
- ☐ _____
- ☐ _____
- ☐ _____
- ☐ _____
- ☐ _____
- ☐ _____
- ☐ _____
- ☐ _____

APPOINTMENTS & MEETINGS

DATE	TIME	VENDOR	PURPOSE

Weekly Wedding Planning

WEEK OF: _____

MONDAY

TUESDAY

WEDNESDAY

THURSDAY

FRIDAY

SATURDAY

WEDDING TO DO LIST

- ☐ _____
- ☐ _____
- ☐ _____
- ☐ _____
- ☐ _____
- ☐ _____
- ☐ _____
- ☐ _____
- ☐ _____
- ☐ _____
- ☐ _____
- ☐ _____
- ☐ _____
- ☐ _____
- ☐ _____
- ☐ _____

APPOINTMENTS & MEETINGS

DATE	TIME	VENDOR	PURPOSE

Weekly Wedding Planning

WEEK OF: _____

MONDAY

TUESDAY

WEDNESDAY

THURSDAY

FRIDAY

SATURDAY

WEDDING TO DO LIST

- ☐ _____
- ☐ _____
- ☐ _____
- ☐ _____
- ☐ _____
- ☐ _____
- ☐ _____
- ☐ _____
- ☐ _____
- ☐ _____
- ☐ _____
- ☐ _____
- ☐ _____
- ☐ _____
- ☐ _____
- ☐ _____
- ☐ _____

APPOINTMENTS & MEETINGS

DATE	TIME	VENDOR	PURPOSE

Weekly Wedding Planning

WEEK OF: _____

MONDAY

TUESDAY

WEDNESDAY

THURSDAY

FRIDAY

SATURDAY

WEDDING TO DO LIST

- ☐ _____
- ☐ _____
- ☐ _____
- ☐ _____
- ☐ _____
- ☐ _____
- ☐ _____
- ☐ _____
- ☐ _____
- ☐ _____
- ☐ _____
- ☐ _____
- ☐ _____
- ☐ _____
- ☐ _____
- ☐ _____
- ☐ _____
- ☐ _____
- ☐ _____

APPOINTMENTS & MEETINGS

DATE	TIME	VENDOR	PURPOSE

Weekly Wedding Planning

WEEK OF: _____

MONDAY

TUESDAY

WEDNESDAY

THURSDAY

FRIDAY

SATURDAY

WEDDING TO DO LIST

- ☐ _____
- ☐ _____
- ☐ _____
- ☐ _____
- ☐ _____
- ☐ _____
- ☐ _____
- ☐ _____
- ☐ _____
- ☐ _____
- ☐ _____
- ☐ _____
- ☐ _____
- ☐ _____
- ☐ _____
- ☐ _____
- ☐ _____

APPOINTMENTS & MEETINGS

DATE	TIME	VENDOR	PURPOSE

Weekly Wedding Planning

WEEK OF: _____

WEDDING TO DO LIST

- [ ] _____
- [ ] _____
- [ ] _____
- [ ] _____
- [ ] _____
- [ ] _____
- [ ] _____
- [ ] _____
- [ ] _____
- [ ] _____
- [ ] _____
- [ ] _____
- [ ] _____
- [ ] _____
- [ ] _____
- [ ] _____

MONDAY

TUESDAY

WEDNESDAY

THURSDAY

FRIDAY

SATURDAY

APPOINTMENTS & MEETINGS

DATE	TIME	VENDOR	PURPOSE

Wedding to do List

Wedding Planning Notes ♡

Wedding Guest List

NAME	ADDRESS	PHONE#	# IN PARTY	RSVP ✔

Wedding Guest List

NAME	ADDRESS	PHONE#	# IN PARTY	RSVP ✔

Wedding Guest List

NAME	ADDRESS	PHONE#	# IN PARTY	RSVP ✔

Wedding Guest List

NAME	ADDRESS	PHONE#	# IN PARTY	RSVP ✔

Wedding Guest List

NAME	ADDRESS	PHONE#	# IN PARTY	RSVP ✔

Wedding Guest List

NAME	ADDRESS	PHONE#	# IN PARTY	RSVP ✔

Wedding Guest List

NAME	ADDRESS	PHONE#	# IN PARTY	RSVP ✔

Wedding Guest List

NAME	ADDRESS	PHONE#	# IN PARTY	RSVP ✔

Wedding Guest List

NAME	ADDRESS	PHONE#	# IN PARTY	RSVP ✔

Wedding Guest List

NAME	ADDRESS	PHONE#	# IN PARTY	RSVP ✔

Wedding Guest List

NAME	ADDRESS	PHONE#	# IN PARTY	RSVP ✔

Wedding Guest List

NAME	ADDRESS	PHONE#	# IN PARTY	RSVP ✔

Wedding Guest List

NAME	ADDRESS	PHONE#	# IN PARTY	RSVP ✔

Wedding Guest List

NAME	ADDRESS	PHONE#	# IN PARTY	RSVP ✔

Wedding Guest List

NAME	ADDRESS	PHONE#	# IN PARTY	RSVP ✔

Wedding Guest List

NAME	ADDRESS	PHONE#	# IN PARTY	RSVP ✔

Wedding Guest List

NAME	ADDRESS	PHONE#	# IN PARTY	RSVP ✔

Wedding Guest List

NAME	ADDRESS	PHONE#	# IN PARTY	RSVP ✔

Wedding Guest List

NAME	ADDRESS	PHONE#	# IN PARTY	RSVP ✔

Wedding Guest List

NAME	ADDRESS	PHONE#	# IN PARTY	RSVP ✔

Wedding Seating Chart

Table #

Table #

love

TABLE #:

1:

2:

3:

4:

5:

6:

7:

8:

TABLE #:

1:

2:

3:

4:

5:

6:

7:

8:

Wedding Seating Chart

Table #

TABLE #:
1:
2:
3:
4:
5:
6:
7:
8:

love

Table #

TABLE #:
1:
2:
3:
4:
5:
6:
7:
8:

Wedding Seating Chart

Table #

TABLE #:
1:
2:
3:
4:
5:
6:
7:
8:

Table #

TABLE #:
1:
2:
3:
4:
5:
6:
7:
8:

Wedding Seating Chart

Table #

TABLE #:

1:

2:

3:

4:

5:

6:

7:

8:

Table #

TABLE #:

1:

2:

3:

4:

5:

6:

7:

8:

Wedding Seating Chart

Table #

Table #

TABLE #:

1:

2:

3:

4:

5:

6:

7:

8:

TABLE #:

1:

2:

3:

4:

5:

6:

7:

8:

Wedding Seating Chart

Table #

TABLE #:
1:
2:
3:
4:
5:
6:
7:
8:

Table #

TABLE #:
1:
2:
3:
4:
5:
6:
7:
8:

Wedding Seating Chart

Table #

TABLE #:
1:
2:
3:
4:
5:
6:
7:
8:

Table #

TABLE #:
1:
2:
3:
4:
5:
6:
7:
8:

Wedding Seating Chart

Table #

TABLE #:
1:
2:
3:
4:
5:
6:
7:
8:

Table #

TABLE #:
1:
2:
3:
4:
5:
6:
7:
8:

Wedding Seating Chart

Table #

TABLE #:
1:
2:
3:
4:
5:
6:
7:
8:

Table #

TABLE #:
1:
2:
3:
4:
5:
6:
7:
8:

Wedding Seating Chart

Table #

TABLE #:
1:
2:
3:
4:
5:
6:
7:
8:

Table #

TABLE #:
1:
2:
3:
4:
5:
6:
7:
8:

Wedding Seating Chart

Table #

TABLE #:
1:
2:
3:
4:
5:
6:
7:
8:

Table #

TABLE #:
1:
2:
3:
4:
5:
6:
7:
8:

Wedding Seating Chart

Table #

TABLE #:
1 :
2 :
3 :
4 :
5 :
6 :
7 :
8 :

Table #

TABLE #:
1 :
2 :
3 :
4 :
5 :
6 :
7 :
8 :

Wedding Seating Chart

Table #

TABLE #:
1:
2:
3:
4:
5:
6:
7:
8:

Table #

TABLE #:
1:
2:
3:
4:
5:
6:
7:
8:

Wedding Seating Chart

Table #

TABLE #:
1:
2:
3:
4:
5:
6:
7:
8:

Table #

TABLE #:
1:
2:
3:
4:
5:
6:
7:
8:

Wedding Seating Chart

Table #

TABLE #:

1:

2:

3:

4:

5:

6:

7:

8:

Table #

TABLE #:

1:

2:

3:

4:

5:

6:

7:

8:

Wedding Seating Chart

Table #

TABLE #:
1:
2:
3:
4:
5:
6:
7:
8:

Table #

TABLE #:
1:
2:
3:
4:
5:
6:
7:
8:

Wedding Seating Chart

Table #

TABLE #:
1:
2:
3:
4:
5:
6:
7:
8:

Table #

TABLE #:
1:
2:
3:
4:
5:
6:
7:
8:

Wedding Seating Chart

Table #

TABLE #:
1:
2:
3:
4:
5:
6:
7:
8:

Table #

TABLE #:
1:
2:
3:
4:
5:
6:
7:
8:

Wedding Seating Chart

Table #

TABLE #:

1:

2:

3:

4:

5:

6:

7:

8:

Table #

TABLE #:

1:

2:

3:

4:

5:

6:

7:

8:

Wedding Seating Chart

Table #

TABLE #:

1:

2:

3:

4:

5:

6:

7:

8:

Table #

TABLE #:

1:

2:

3:

4:

5:

6:

7:

8:

Wedding Seating Chart

Table #

TABLE #:
1:
2:
3:
4:
5:
6:
7:
8:

Table #

TABLE #:
1:
2:
3:
4:
5:
6:
7:
8:

Wedding Seating Chart

Table #

TABLE #:

1:

2:

3:

4:

5:

6:

7:

8:

Table #

TABLE #:

1:

2:

3:

4:

5:

6:

7:

8:

Wedding Seating Chart

Table #

TABLE #:

1:

2:

3:

4:

5:

6:

7:

8:

Table #

TABLE #:

1:

2:

3:

4:

5:

6:

7:

8:

Wedding Seating Chart

Table #

TABLE #:
1:
2:
3:
4:
5:
6:
7:
8:

Table #

TABLE #:
1:
2:
3:
4:
5:
6:
7:
8:

Wedding Seating Chart

Table #

TABLE #:

1:

2:

3:

4:

5:

6:

7:

8:

Table #

TABLE #:

1:

2:

3:

4:

5:

6:

7:

8:

Wedding Seating Chart

Table

TABLE #:

1:	2:	3:	4:	5:	6:	7:	8:
9:	10:	11:	12:	13:	14:	15:	16:

Table

TABLE #:

1:	2:	3:	4:	5:	6:	7:	8:
9:	10:	11:	12:	13:	14:	15:	16:

Wedding Seating Chart

Table

TABLE #:

1:	2:	3:	4:	5:	6:	7:	8:
9:	10:	11:	12:	13:	14:	15:	16:

Table

TABLE #:

1:	2:	3:	4:	5:	6:	7:	8:
9:	10:	11:	12:	13:	14:	15:	16:

Wedding Seating Chart

Table

TABLE #:

1:	2:	3:	4:	5:	6:	7:	8:
9:	10:	11:	12:	13:	14:	15:	16:

Table

TABLE #:

1:	2:	3:	4:	5:	6:	7:	8:
9:	10:	11:	12:	13:	14:	15:	16:

Wedding Seating Chart

Table

TABLE #:

1:	2:	3:	4:	5:	6:	7:	8:
9:	10:	11:	12:	13:	14:	15:	16:

Table

TABLE #:

1:	2:	3:	4:	5:	6:	7:	8:
9:	10:	11:	12:	13:	14:	15:	16:

Wedding Seating Chart

Table #

TABLE #:							
1:	2:	3:	4:	5:	6:	7:	8:
9:	10:	11:	12:	13:	14:	15:	16:

Table #

TABLE #:							
1:	2:	3:	4:	5:	6:	7:	8:
9:	10:	11:	12:	13:	14:	15:	16:

Wedding Seating Chart

Table #

TABLE #:

1:	2:	3:	4:	5:	6:	7:	8:
9:	10:	11:	12:	13:	14:	15:	16:

Table #

TABLE #:

1:	2:	3:	4:	5:	6:	7:	8:
9:	10:	11:	12:	13:	14:	15:	16:

Wedding Seating Chart

Table #

TABLE #:

1:	2:	3:	4:	5:	6:	7:	8:
9:	10:	11:	12:	13:	14:	15:	16:

Table #

TABLE #:

1:	2:	3:	4:	5:	6:	7:	8:
9:	10:	11:	12:	13:	14:	15:	16:

Wedding Seating Chart

Table

TABLE #:

1:	2:	3:	4:	5:	6:	7:	8:
9:	10:	11:	12:	13:	14:	15:	16:

Table

TABLE #:

1:	2:	3:	4:	5:	6:	7:	8:
9:	10:	11:	12:	13:	14:	15:	16:

Wedding Seating Chart

Table

TABLE #:

1:	2:	3:	4:	5:	6:	7:	8:
9:	10:	11:	12:	13:	14:	15:	16:

Table

TABLE #:

1:	2:	3:	4:	5:	6:	7:	8:
9:	10:	11:	12:	13:	14:	15:	16:

Wedding Seating Chart

Table

TABLE #:

1:	2:	3:	4:	5:	6:	7:	8:
9:	10:	11:	12:	13:	14:	15:	16:

Table

TABLE #:

1:	2:	3:	4:	5:	6:	7:	8:
9:	10:	11:	12:	13:	14:	15:	16:

Wedding Seating Chart

Table

TABLE #:

1:	2:	3:	4:	5:	6:	7:	8:
9:	10:	11:	12:	13:	14:	15:	16:

Table

TABLE #:

1:	2:	3:	4:	5:	6:	7:	8:
9:	10:	11:	12:	13:	14:	15:	16:

Wedding Seating Chart

Table

TABLE #:

1:	2:	3:	4:	5:	6:	7:	8:
9:	10:	11:	12:	13:	14:	15:	16:

Table

TABLE #:

1:	2:	3:	4:	5:	6:	7:	8:
9:	10:	11:	12:	13:	14:	15:	16:

Love

Best Wishes

Made in the USA
Monee, IL
08 January 2021